THE
REALITIES
OF THE
Bafut
Kingdom

———— ◆ ————

JOHN MABO

The Realities of the Bafut Kingdom

iUniverse books may be ordered through booksellers or by contacting:

iUniverse
1663 Liberty Drive
Bloomington, IN 47403
www.iuniverse.com
844-349-9409

ISBN: 978-1-6632-1476-8 (sc)
ISBN: 978-1-6632-1477-5 (e)

Library of Congress Control Number: 2020924740

Print information available on the last page.

iUniverse rev. date: 01/26/2021

CONTENTS

Before the coming of white civilization to Bafut, the society had an organized hierarchical form that functioned very well based on their traditional religion which nurtures their culture. At the end of colonial rule, and with the emergence of independent modern states,which reflected imperialistic tendencies, His Royal Highness the Fon, the traditional institutions and the traditional religion were apparently wakened but nevertheless, the culture of the Bafut people, their tradition and the traditional religion of the ancestors remains intact and not only very powerful and imposing but also impacting. The progress of history from the colonial period to the emergence of independent states alienated a majority of Bafut people with their tradition and the aspiration of the ancestors. This because the modern christainity frowned on everything traditional as it was considered paganic and thus very distant from God. This was greatly admired by the majority of the indigenes, some completely cutting off all communication or anything traditional. This created the missing link and brought misfortune and even death to many Bafut people who neither fully belonged to the foreign culture that derailed them nor to their own which has its roots with their ancestors, who are very concerned with their progress in their specificity. The missing link is the principal motivation behind this write up which intends to help the Bafut people get back to their roots and be empowered to attain prominence which is the general aspiration of the ancestors.

For a better understanding of the traditions and aspirations of the ancestors which culminates in our culture we would attempt a vivid descriptions of the structures of the Bafut society and the interaction between the various setups and individuals. In this attempt we are presenting the feelings of ours ancestor and hence how these are transgressed and the subsequent boomerang effect.

HIS ROYAL HIGHNESS THE FON OF BAFUT

His Royal Highness the Fon of Bafut is the first personality, representative of the ancestors, symbol of the tradition and the supreme ruler of the Bafut dynasty. These powers are handed over to him at the disappearance of his father into the spirit world, followed by the official enthronement ceremony. This ceremony is officiated by the government in view of its importance. He is invested with monarchical powers. All the Bafut people participate in crowning him by shooting him with stones not to hurt but to empower him to be above all and all powerful. It is compulsory for all to participate in this ceremony and all the societies existing in Bafut are also compelled to participate or loose their credibility. All Bafut people come to the ceremony covering their perineal areas with plantain leaves with nothing covering the entire body as a sign of mourning. All the princesses come out without anything covering any part of their bodies, as a sign of mourning. All are expected to be mourning without laughter, mockry or fun. After crowning the Fon, he inherits his fathers mobile and immobile assets including wives and children. The Fon does not dowry a woman and has the right to marry as many wives as he can. The more women the Fon has, the greater his dignity.

The dignity of the Fon can be noticed during occasions, especially in the palace. When everyone is well seated and waiting, one of the Fon's musicians would come out and announce his coming with a trumpet sound. Everyone would respond by rising up and you can see the Fon gorgeously dressed and moving majestically among a crowd and His attire proclaiming Him.If it is too sunny or rainy one of His attendance would shade Him with an umbrela. And all His wives are moving around Him, well dressed, with frequent incantations in praise of His Royal Highness[HRH]. For example, suddenly, one of the delighted wives would shout,',eh eh e e e le le le le le,'and the others would respond, 'ho a a a e e e ei, 'then she would retort one of the following, among many, acha ngwo kwake,cha abue, meaning when he passes by, fowls cry out, and above all people.

When finally HRH is well seated, surrounded by His wives, followed by second class chiefs and the Fon's advisers and notables. One of His wives is holding a well decorated calabash containing the Fon's palm wine, ready to pour it into His cup whenever He needs it.Then you can notice people dressed in traditional attire come up to the Fon, bow down before Him, clap their hands cover their mouths with their hands, greet the Fon, chat with Him for a while then go away for the others to do same.This continues for sometime before the start of the occasion.

PREVILEDGES OF THE FON

The Fon has a lot of previledges,as defined by our ancestors in the unwritten constitution defined by the ancestors. The population is reminded of this aspect of the previledges of the FON and the need for love and wellbeing for all in the form of a pledge which is rhetorically sung by the entire population at the start of each occasion. The meaning of this pledge, which is known as mban will be explained later.The following are the previledges of HRH the Fon of Bafut.

THE FON'S CORONATION RIGHT

The Fon has the right to coronate only one second class Chief or Atancho in his life time. This is intended to eliminate conflict of interest .The Fon will not choose anyone for the post until he has proved his worth in the form of material provision. The existence of a vacancy for an Atancho will undoubtedly provide many bidders and the highest bidder might be the winner, except otherwise. However no matter the circumstance as soon as the traditional coronation ceremony has taken place, the situation will never be altered. It is very pertinent to note here that anyone who challenges the authority of the Fon should be prepared to face the wrath of the ancestors. Those who do not succeed in such a bid should politely approach the Fon and they could be named a quarter head and this could subsequently lead to being named Atancho, in view of good works.

THE FON'S SPECIAL PALMWINE

The Fon's calabash of wine is not expected to be empty, because the thirst and annoyance of the Fon can bring misfortune to the people.For this reason in every village, there is a specified circumscription for the Fons taper and a taper is appointed and the best wine producing tree is assigned to him for the sole purpose of producing the Fon's wine.Any owner who opposes is sanctioned. When the taper produce the wine, he takes it to the palace in a specially covered calabash, communicating with no body on the way to deliver the palm wine.

THE FON'S FARMS

The Fon and the family are not expected to be hungry because,just as mentioned before, this would bring misfortune to the people. This explains why the entire population of Bafut participate in the Fons's farms. All participate in land preparation, farming, weeding and harvesting..The best farmlands are reserved for this purpose and all villages are assigned specific dates for the purpose.The best inputs are expected from all in order to have the best output. Maybe this explains why the princess and princesses are very healthy and strong.

BWI INFOR

There are houses in the palace that are supposed to be roofed only with grass. There is a season during which the entire population is expected to supply the palace with grass for this purpose. All the men of each village are obliged to cut grass from specified hills and not only bring it to the palace but arrange it in identified places for each village for easy appreciation to facilitate the price giving ceremony officiated by HRH, the Fon at the end of year festivities.

ME INFOR

This is the most important traditioinal religious ceremony as it links the present and the past. After crowning the Fon, he becomes a reservoir of the traditional values of the Bafut Fondom .This gives the Fon an unchallengeable authority and immunity that places him above everybody present in the Bafut territory. This is manifested by the fact that the Fon is not allowed to greet anybody with his hands in the Bafut territory, applicable to both indigenes and foreigners.. No indigene is allowed to talk to the Fon until he/ she has gone through the me infor process . The following is a description of the process and its significance, There comes a time in every Bafut man's life when he/she feels that it is time for him /her to be able to communicate with the Fon directly.. This is the case because one might have pertinent issues to discuss with the Fon but barred by the fact that it is not possible to discuss with the Fon because the me infor ceremony had not been performed, There are also other important issues that one cannot transact without having gone through the me infor ceremony Just like the successor ship ceremony, every mumita, which is the traditiona Sunday, the Fon is seated on his throne . under the plum tree besides the most important shrine in the palace, By means of appointment . those who have fulfilled the requirements come in .on call for the ceremony and goes down on the knees before the Fon and the Fon proceeds to robe the fore face with calm wood and permits the concerned to drink from the royal cup but not directly from the cup but through wrapped hands around the mouth,

The significance of this ceremony focuses on what we call the missing link between the past and the present or otherwise the connection between ancestral values which as blessings to the receiver are capable of healing protecting and promoting,

With these advantages of the mi infor ceremony well explained in the Bafut traditional religion. we can understand why the imperialist understands that the tradition is what empowers the people and the best way of weakening them is to take them away from this tradition, That explains why they call our traditional rituals paganic and should be abandoned. There arose the conflict between modernism and tradition and every critical observer should by now conclude that modernism is not meant to promote the African but to robe them of their privileges.

MBO OH

In the Bafut tradition .when the family extends to a point where confusion can arise from the sharing of things especially in marriages the concept called mbo oh automatically cuts off some members of the family. This also provides a good line of demarcation in the legal concept of incest .

In some families the ceremony is carried out in the streets but in the absence of this ceremony the link is supposed to cut instantly. The illustration here is that your parents cousins are not expected to participate in your children's dowry ceremonies.

THE FON'S IMMUNITY

The Fon has the immunity of the dignity and respect handed to him or inherited by him from his parents who link him to the other ancestors .For this reason just like his parents, HRH does not greet anybody no matter the level with the hand. His annoyance, insult or slap would result in a curse to the person concerned. Hence if the Fon is annoyed or insults you, go down on your knees and apologise immediately or if he slaps you, do same and make sure you touch him to neutralize the effects. There are living evidences to these facts, hence to be informed is to be protected.

THE FON IS THE REPRESENTATIVE OF HIS PEOPLE

The Fon represents his people internally and externally. Externally he does this in all matters concerning other territories and internally he represents all his people irrespective of language, race, religion and in his political opinion. This explains why he refers to himself as the father of all and not only welcomes but hosts all political parties as the father of all. He makes a tour of all the villages to acquaint himself with his people and their problems.

THE FON IS AN AUXILLARY OF THE ADMINISTRATION

The government recognizes the Fon as a civil administrator. This is inherited from the colonial rule when the British colonial masters administered the people indirectly through the Fon. They realized that the people were very submisive to their Fon and they went ahead to govern the people through the Fon. The Fon is paid as an auxiliary of the administration as well as all the second class chiefs for the civil administration duties they perform. This facilitates the administrative task by making it possible for directives to reach the periphery.

THE OBLIGATIONS OF THE FON

The Fon is the protector of all the Bafut people without distinction to age, sex or belief. This explains why all the Fons of Bafut have always declared that they are non- partisan. All shades of opinion converge in the palace because the Fon is the father of all. He receives all people on mumita and is always very keen on all problems concerning everybody. The Fon in collaboration with some institutions are always there to provide solutions to all the problem s of everybody..

The Fon is responsible for the appreciation of merit by giving titles to all those who defend the territorial integrity, had academic accomplishments, political accomplishments and other traditional accomplishments. This comes in the form of graded attachments to the traditional cap e.g red feather etc. The recipients celebrate the importance of this with their people.

HRH the Fon is the physical link between the ancestors and the present generation and is therefore expected to use his good offices to protect the true values of the society which are the general aspirations of the ancestors but difficult to nurture. These true values are difficult to identify because evil values are always highly embellished, apparently good and forcefully pushed through by the strong majority who are interested in nothing but their self interest and self aggrandizement . Nevertheless these egoistic ones find their dreadful end after a short lifespan because the ancestors, who are in the spirit world, never waste time to frustrate those who want to put an end to the advancement of true values which is the equivalence of the advancement of society and the liberation of the people .

Some Administrative Institutions of the Bafut Kingdom

There are many Administrative institutions including the following;

KWIIFOR

This name identifies kwiifor as the one that babysits the Fon. This is the highest organ that assists the Fon in all Administrative and legal matters. It is a closed and masculin society whose members must not be princess or women. As soon as the scary sound of kwiifor is heard, pandamonium breaks loose, and everybody goes into hiding for the following reasons. It is strickly forbiden for non -initiated men and all women to see kwiifor and if one does so, there are serious consequences. Kwiifor is responsible for the burial of princes and princessess and other important personalities in the community. Huge sums of money are spent for kwiifor to realize this and perform other traditional rites in the funeral. Kwiifor is also responsible for libations in the important shrines in the entire Bafut kingdom.

JOONG

Joong is made up of princes and very important princesses. It is a highly closed society that is always with the Fon, advising him how to govern the territory. After kwiifor has gone for the burial of whoever, the next day Joong also goes there only for the family to continue in huge expenses. When Joong goes out, nobody is permited to see it except initiated ones and no gun shot is allowed.

There are two institutions that are closely linked to the Fon viz;

ACHU_UNKAA . This is the Fon's secret heart society, made up of very close people to the Fon, who take care of him.

NDANSIE, They are also very closely linked to the Fon but their functions are not very clear. Nevertheless they must be people who have reached alevel of maturity.

TAKUMBENG. This is a highly closed society only for princes. Their principal function is the development and wellbeing of the entire Bafut population. They are the deacons of the Bafut traditional religion. They are responsible for constructing the traditional god houses in the central community fields of each village. This is done in November each year, which is known as the takumeng period. It is beleived that ancestral gods and takumbeng stay in that house and supervise development projectsthat take place in each village. The central or headquarter takumbeng shrine is the first shrine in the Palace that welcomes one from Nsanimunwi. This is the one that empowers all others. When they come out for such activities, they have the right to eat whatever they want. Thus nobody complains that his plaintain is harvested or his \her fowl or goat is caugjht by takumbeng. The village quarterheads are responsible for their palm wine.

CENTRAL MANJONG. This is the headquarters of Manjong situated in the palace. Manjong is the general meeting of all the Bafut people irrespective of age, sex, religion, social status or orientation for the purpose of development and the promotion of the Bafut culture sand the welbeing of all Bafut people. This meeting, which was inspired by the ancestors, was initiated by some Bafut elites and elders in the early seventies .Manjong has successfully established everywhere in Cameroon and abroad. It is working incredibly well in development and others are not only admiring but emulating this good example. The unifying force of Manjong is based on the Bafut proverb which states that [aafaah achwie bi-ieh] meaning that we are the ones who are here, i-e unity is the force that keeps us alive. This proverb was used by the ancestors who went to foreign lands and realized that, they could better solve their problems as a group than an an individual. Hence all Bafut people are obliged to be members of Manjong whether they are in Bafut or abroad and are expected to work together to bridge the missing link so as to usher ancestral blessings because working together in genuine iove, attracts good ancestors who protect and empower all to prominence.

In order to have a of clearer picture of who the Bafut people are and also have a better appreciation of the context in which they live, it is worthwhile briefly describing the land they occupy. This might help in suggesting advancement possibilities.

The Bafut population is settled in a highly privileged and large piece of land that comprises savannah highlands and semi coastal fertile area. The savannah highlands have easy accessible hills and lowland watershed areas with flowing streams that provide a lot of fertile farmlands and resources in these flowing streams and on their banks. The highlands, blessed with trees are good sources of water supply through pipelines moved by pressure to tanks that provide good water supply for some of the villages, e.g the Mankaha and Niko water supply projects that have provided pure drinking water to Central Bafut at a minimal cost.The most common tree to be found on these highlands is the palm tree, planted mostly by rodents and the raffia palm trees which provide good resources for the serious individuals .

Concerning the description of Bafut as a semi –coastal fertile piece of land, the following points can be raised; The lowlands of Bafut have the same characteristics as coastal lands because of the large river flowing through it. The three large rivers that flow through Bafut take their rises from Mezam, Big Babanki and Kom, and flow throw the unexploited forest and converge in the lowlands, forming the large river that flows throw the entire lowlands providing very fertile soil for farmlands which are cultivated throughout the year, when there is no severe rainfall.All good farmers in Bamenda struggle to have farmlands in this lowland because it is very fertile with high yield in everything that does well in the coastal lands.

Bafut has a heterogeneous population .Some people settled in lower Bafut speak different dialets from others spoken in Bafut.The reason for this is because they have different origins.

A BRIEF HISTORY OF THE ORIGINAL SETTLERS IN BAFUT

This is only an indicative presentation which should provoke genuine research into the the origins of the various villages in Bafut. This information is available with the elders of each village . It is worthwhile understanding it because genuine development can take place if only the past, present and future are harmonized. It is stated that the first settlers in Bafut came from various places notably Ngoketungia, North Cameroon, Kom and many otherplaces. The movement of people to distant lands was to avoid wars fought by warriors who came on horse back, fighting everybody with an aim of defeating everyone and accumulating wealth for themselves. For the sake of security, people moved in groups and settled in the same group in places where they felt were more secured. They usually recognized one person as their leader and settled under him in their small cluster. The first meeting of the leaders of the groups that settled in the North or upper Bafut took place in Mbebeli which later became known as Mbah. These leaders formed their first union so that they could discuss and solve their problems together. Their principal concern was to be able to fight the enemy together as a stronger force. Therefore they made a pledge to block themselves in the union called [Biifeu] and with time this became known as Bafut. In this same union of the leaders, they agreed to use one language. They brought all their people together under the ruler who was the all powerful who had to take care of all people and having monarchical powers. The people had to respect and support the leader so that he would in turn be able to support the others. They made a pledge to respect this in a song called mban. This will be examined later.

THE ORIGIN OF THE CONFLICT BETWEEN
THE FON OF BAFUT AND THE CHIEF OF BAWUM

This is a problem that has existed from the time of Mbah until today. The Head of the Mbah group was the leader of the Bawum people . He was very greedy and did not want to share with others. This was contrary to the peoples culture and mban and as a result everybody was very annoyed with him. On the contrary the leader who served them in the inner circle was an open man who shared with everyone. His behavior attracted the admiration of all the other leaders .They started planning together and finally instructed the servant to usurp the leader by stepping on his toes when he is in the process of serving wine. Their plan materialized as he continued with his greed without knowing. As soon as the servant collected the things at the door and moved into the house, he pretended as if he was falling and stepped on the toes of their leader and unanimously all shouted, why have you stepped on the toes of the leader ? Traditionally, you have seized the powers from the leader and you must be made the ruler, and immediately the crown was forcefully put on his head and was officially installed as the new leader. As the days went by his administration was so good that everybody admired him. However, the dethroned became very annoyed and was envisioning a plan to eliminate him. This was the most disturbing news and everyone was thinking of how to avoid this from happening.

One of the mothers in the newly crowned leader's family, went out one day in search of excellent fishing rivers. She followed the flowing stream until she arrived at the river junction close to the present Bafut palace. After preparing the water for a catch, she decided to go upland to discover what it looked like. And behold, she arrived at a level piece of land, which, unlike the stony hills they are presently occupying was a level piece of land, without stones, that was an excellent settlement. This could be the best settlement for my people, she thought and when she arrived home she informed the new leader and elders and immediately the elders went down there and when they saw the beauty of the land, they immediately packed their things, went down and settled there. The place became known as Bujong and they constructed their palace there and all their families came down and settled where we now call Mbebali in the center of Bafut. The leader who moved down and settled in Bujong is the ancestor of the present Fon of Bafut. The antagonism that existed between the ancestor of the leader of the Bawum people and the ancestor of the Bujong leader continued until today. When the new leader of Mbah finally left Mbah, all the other groups also left and settled in different places, either still in Bafut or further away, e.g, the Nkwen Fon took his people to where they are now settled.

Before the ancestors who settled in Bujong came down, there were already settled in Central Bafut,the Niko and the Njibujang people .The relics of these earlier settlements can be found in the Ntomunwis that are found in these two villages. These were formally points for traditional rituals but with the coming of the Ntonwis these have been harmonized in one place. This will be highlighted later. The new leader at Bujong was very powerful and had a great number of people and warriors. They eventually subdued the Niko and NJibujang people and controlled them in every aspect. Nevertheless at one point when the Niko people realized that the new leader was more powerful and was cheating them in every aspect, they packed their things and set off for another destination. When news reached the Bujong palace that the Niko people were moving away, they sent mabu who bypassed them and laid across the road traditionally prohibiting them from going. The Niko people had no choice than to respect the tradition and go back. The Fon then understood that he had to handle the Niko people with care.

THE FIELD OF GOD'S CHILD

The Fon had very powerful people who helped him to subdue not only the Njko and Njibujang people but all the other surrounding villages that make up the Bafut Fondom or dynasty . They regarded their coming down as a blessing and everybody realized that if they were still in the north, their leader would have been killed. The virtuous people of the society started lavishing praises on the woman who discovered the land and brought them down . This was very disappointing to other people who, out of envy, saw her as a threat to their own position. The praises given to the lady were those that ought to qualify her for one of the highest positions in the Fondom . The vicious people told the Fon that his position as Fon was threatened if this woman was allowed to continue living. They forced the Fon to believe that if she were allowed to live, she would replace him after his death. The Fon pondered for a while and enquired from them what they wanted him to do to stop her from going further because she seemed to be going too fast. In an effort to amplify their point, they reiterated the fact that everybody seemed to be talking about her boldness, wisdom and foresight. They told the Fon without mincing words that she should be secretly enticed into destruction. The reaction of the Fon at first was very negative. He reprimanded them in a declaration that what they were saying is not correct because it might have a negative impact on him. They went away and came back to the Fon with a more convincing version which was rhetoric because they used the good offices of kwifor in a manner that it became imperative for the Fon to accept.

Thus, with the endorsement of the Fon, nkwifor then officially informed the lady concerned that they were going to officially crown her Ma allaah at a place very close to the palace, on a specific date. They promised to build for her a beautiful residence at same venue. They then secretly went ahead and dug a very deep pit and covered it with very fragile sticks and decorated it, with a beautiful seat on it. She was informed that everything was ready for the party. And behold, when she innocently came to the scene, she was shown her seat and she could not believe her eyes, especially as they were very few people concerned. Nevertheless, she felt so dignified and thus in great expectation proudly advanced to occupy the crown. As soon as she put her weight on the crown, everything collapsed and took her into the pit and she was buried alive. The crime was too heavy on them and they named her munwi, as they regretted that she was killed innocently. And the spot on which she was killed became known as nsanimunwi, meaning,' the field of Gods child.' That spot became a nightmare as this innocently killed lady was found seating on her grave and molesting everybody around the environment for centuries until the coming of the ntonwis who mitigated with offerings. She became known as ndi allah mbwe. The ntonwis advised that the successor of this woman be named and a ceremony for her. The question still remains unanswered as to whether the right successor was named and the ceremony conducted.

Until the nineteen seventies, Nsanimunwi used to be a very dangerous place where people used to fight and go as far as stabbing each other with knives. It has been explained by the ntonwis that this and many other terrible things that happen in Bafut are caused by this lady. When the Ntonwis emerged, they had no choice than to singlehandedly handle some of these issues such as making sacrifices for these aggrieved spirits to go away. THE BAFUT POPULATION IN LATER YEARS.

As time progressed, the various settlers in Bafut realized that they had no choice than to respect the authority of the Fon of Bafut who was officially crowned by the ancestors and with his various warriors they defeated all the other settlers, no matter from where they came. The different settlers subsequently developed into villages with their leaders as second class chiefs. In this present circumstance, two distinct groups of people emerged in the Bafut society viz;Buntoh and Bangong. Buntoh are the princes and princesses and Bangong are those who do not come from the palace. The Buntohs feel that they are a superior set of people because they belong to the family of the Fon who is above all people. Nevertheless they have some previledges which justifies their superiority complex but that notwithstanding, they are not better than any other person in Bafut. Some of the previledges of Buntohs include,inter alia,they are fed by the entire community by the food harvested from the Fon's farms and when they become of age and ready to build, they are given land by the constituted authorities and they only have to mobllise resources to construct their houses with the support of the Fon.As princes and princesses, they belong to either Joong or Takumbeng. Each time they go out for anything,like deaths they are paid large sums of money. The death of a prince or princesses is the sole prerogative nkwifor and the other princes and princesses to bury and officiate in the funeral proceedings .This is done with very huge expenses which have rendered many people bankrupt. And the cycle continues because when they die the same thing is done . Therefore they have not only enough to eat but are also provided with land on which to build. This has permitted many of them to become polygamists with many children. This has created a superiority complex syndrome which have adverse retrogressive effects on Buntohs themselves and their significant others, eventhough they would never accept it.

The other class of people who exist in the Bafut society are the Bangong. They are the principal ones on whom the economy and many other aspects of the society depend. More than eighty percent of the population are farmers. There is real competition in which each parent tries as much as possible to send his children to the best colleges. This has resulted in a lot of educated youths and many of them having doctorate degrees. The women are mostly involved in farming on the highlands and the watershed areas concentrating on cassava, colocatia or ibo coco, beans,maize ginger and a variety of yams etc .The men are involved in livestock and tapping . A majority of Bafut men are involved in harnessing the palm tree, which is the commonest tree in Bafut, mostly planted by rodents in the forest. A majority of men endeavor to sell at least a jug of palm wine everyday for three thousand FCFA, spend one thousand for his daily contribution, one thousand for food and one thousand reserved for the beer parlor in the night where he would project his manhood.In the evening people always go to the beer parlor to either buy, beg or borrow a bottle of beer to talk away the evening in amusement. Here, follows an example of a dialog in a bar in Nsanimunwi. There are two Buntoh;s sitting very close to the entrance of the bar, each rtelaxing with a bottle of beer.l Many others are seated all round inside chating very closely, each with a bottle of beer in front of him. The prominent themes to be identified in their conversation is based on highly assertive claims of importance, bravery or wisdom of each one. Suddenly Che Cletus, a young man who had gone to the southwest or the coast entered the bar, looking so fresh and neatly dressed. He greeted the Buntohs who were sitting at a very conspicuous place. They responded and enquired from him when he came and Che replied that he came three days ago. One of them remarked in an assertive manner that, how can you come three days ago and I am seeing you now. Don't you know that when you were in the coast I was taking care of your old father? And he continued that, all the same get for us two bottles of beer as a sign of appreciation. The man sitting next to them shouted, welcome Mr Che embraced him, emptied his bottle of beer in his glass and said, 'let me welcome you with this.' This was intended to lure him into buying for him a bottle of beer. Mr Che refused and continued to the counter, ordered for bottle of beer, which was opened and handed over to him. He immediately lifted his head up and poured about one third of the contents of the bottle in his mouth. And another man shouted,' what is happening to these young people, you must pay a fine, you drank the head mimbo eventhough there are your superiors in the house. Everybody in the bar supported him and it became a very serious matter until he ordered for a crate of beer which was divided to all, some having one bottle and others sharing. This became an issue because the tradition requires the respect of seniors . He was expected to give first to the seniors before consuming it. He was expected to pour some of his beer into a senior's cup or order drinks for some seniors before satisfying himself. As they were happily drinking their beer, one of the muntohs asked the man sitting closest to him, I heard you asking Che why he did not pour the head mimbo into your cup, if he gave you in my presence would you take, just the same as you would take the gills of the chicken when I am present.

THE CEREMONIES IN THE LIVES OF THE BAFUT PEOPLE

THE NFEH CEREMONY

When a Prince turns twenty one years old, he is expected to go out of the palace and settle in his own compound. Traditionally the welfare of everyone is the concern of the entire family. Thus at the agreed date, every Prince is expected to announce to the family that he is ready to move out of the palace, and settle in his own compound. When this happens, the Fon is expected to convene the family to come out with donations to support their brother. There is a compulsory cash donation from all the family members and also food and wine donations to facilitate the feast which takes place in the palace, assisted greatly by the Fon himself. The Fon, in the position of the father, is not expected to be working and earning a salary. The entire population is expected to support the him financially so that he can in turn support the weak and also be able to administer. A recent good example of the Fons lavish support of the weak is the case of Singsaah, one of the weak Princes whose nfeh was where everybody donated generously with the Fon donating the highest amount to support him because he is weak and unable to work .

BIRTH

Birth in the Bafut tradition is a highly recognized ceremony in the family because the child is an extension of the parent and consequently great joy for all. Therefore the birth of a child is a moment of cerebration. The husband is expected to show his manhood and appreciation by making the home comfortable to welcome the new baby. The woman who has gone through a nine months stressful gestation period is to rest after the birth of a baby. Hence her mother or other family members would stay with her for at least one or two months in order to stabilize her. This is the approximated period of festivities during which people come every day to celebrate . Traditionally the husband is compelled to buy at least one tin of oil or two and there must be enough plantains, meat and wine at all times in the house so that everybody who comes for the born house would celebrate as expected.

MARRIAGE

Marriage in the Bafut tradition is the greatest joy and honor for both the families of the bride and the groom. For the family of the bride, if their daughter is not beautiful and well behaved, nobody would marry her . And their honor is underlined by the fact that if they had not raised their child in a good way, nobody would marry her. On the other hand, the joy and honor of the groom's parents is that if they had not raised their son well he would not have been in a of position responsibility that would enable him to be able to marry. There is no single parent who would like to witness the suffering of the children as such they would like to know the family background of the choice in marriage. This explains why many years ago it was compulsory for parents to choose spouses for their children.

However, nowadays marriage always takes the following steps courtship, engagement, introduction to parents, knock door, payment of dowry and finally marriage ceremony, starting with traditional marriage followed by legal marriage and finally church marriage.

COURTSHIP

This is the wooing stage in which the man initiates the action and tactfully plans and executes a familiarization program n of luring her into companionship. To accomplish this he must present the best side of his manhood by means of giving concessions to her. He might do everything to discover what she likes best and do everything as a man to provide her with this at all times. Some females might at first be indifferent but nevertheless this attitude will be touching her in the innermost. She is most probably praying in hiding that he should propose marriage to her. Before this happens she would want to understand his background .He ought to be somebody on whom she could depend; for instance what is his educational background or his job placement, which would enable them to build a house, buy a car and be able to sponsor the children in best schools. These are the desires of the modern girls .In those days the girls preferred men who were powerful, responsible and hardworking. And above all they want men who are presentable with whom they could move around in pride.If all these points are put together, they would become too close and one of them, specifically the boy would improvise a means of always meeting her.

ENGAGEMENT AND INTRODUCTION TO PARENTS

As they become too close, the boy would plan an engagement. This involves only two of them. The manner of doing it depends on the individual. But most specifically it involves an exchange of rings for the present day guys. Many years ago the parents arranged for the marriage and bring them together as virgins and teach them how to consummate love. In the case of the modern day marriage,after the engagement, they would plan to visit their both parents depending on their choices.The visit always affects most parents with mixed feelings such that they would go out on serious investigation of the family history of the concerned family. This is intended to avoid misfortune emanating from the traditional adage that like father like son.

KNOCK DOOR AND CONFIRMATION

The joy of every parent is to be a living witness to the maturity and responsibility of their offspring as expressed in their marriage. Thus the parent of the boy would continously remind him of what to do and as soon as he indicates that he is ready, they would proceed as follows. They would plan together and send word to the family of the girl that they are coming to their compound. On the pla nned date they take some palm wine with them to their in-laws. This, they do in the absence of the boy . The girl is not even expected to be at home. Her parents might have discussed that with her and this is only done as a matter of tradition. If this is a good plan, he would immediately order for the wine to be served so that they would be drinking while waiting for the wife to serve food. As they are joyfully refreshing and discussing, the subject matter would be handled in the conversation, especially in the form of parables,eg we have come to plant a tree in your house.And the conversation would advance in that direction to end on a positive note.

On the contrary if the girl's father is opposed to the idea, he would refuse that the wine should not be drank in his house. This would bring untold frustration especially in the case where the lovers have an unfathomable desire for each other.

If the wine is drank, the boy's father would pay it with a significant amount of money for example five thousand or ten thousand FCFA . Each thousand represents one hundred thousand Francs CFA .In this way he should immediately understand the dowry for his wife. When you marry a woman from Bafut, you become part of that family. This explains why it is difficult to find a case in which someone pays the wine with an amount up to five thousand. Even the highly educated ones hardly have a dowry of more than three hundred thousand FCFA.

The next meeting known as the confirmation stage includes the lovers. In this instance, the parents of the suitor bring descent palm wine, beer and food. When they are at the climax, everybody eating and drinking, he would suddenly call her and ask her, to the hearing of everybody, whether what he is hearing is true and that being the case she should take his cup from his hands, pour some of the palm wine in the calabash, drink some and give the rest to the person she wants to marry. When this is done, it is to the applause of everyone, clapping hands in total jubilation that their child, brother, or cousin has married and very soon they would have grand children,nephews\nieces, and cousins

The parents of the boy at this point feel proud and are ready to do whatever thing is required to complete the process. First of all they are willing to pay immediately or later what was symbolically demanded from them the first day they came for the knock door ceremony. Then they enquire from the inlaws what they are expected to do. They are officially informed about the bride price which had been symbolized, and all they are expected to do as concerns the feeding of the aunts and their compensation including the uncles. They are then informed that after all this has been done, they are free to proceed with the marriage ceremony. After consultations at the levels of the lovers and their parents, there then follows the marriage ceremony. We are concerned only with the traditional marriage because the churc marriage and that at the civil status registry is outside this domain.

THE TRADITIONAL MARRIAGE

The day on which the traditional marriage takes place is a day of pride, joy and festivities for the both families. The entire family of the groom comes to the residence of the bride, very determined to defend themselves as the real successful husband of the beautiful choice they made. The program starts with serious refreshment with a lot of wine, beer, food, meat and other delicacies. The payment of dowry is done in private so that the entire population present does not understand.

The real traditional marriage is done by a responsible member of the bride's family in a conspicuous place so that all can witness. The substance used is palm oil in well decorated jar. The family member officiating the ceremony calls the bride who appears in a beautiful skirt, exposing the upper part but covering her breast .He makes a traditional prayer in which he makes reference to the ancestors and the desire of the whole family to bless her in a successful marriage. He makes a plea to her to genuinely represent the family and to be obedient so that she can have God's blessing so as to multiply good offspring. He then proceeds to robe her with the palm oil so much that her entire body is glinting with oil. At that point he declares that they can take away their wife. Immediately the ladies of the grooms family rush out and delightedly shout out oh o o o o o le le le le le and the others respond o o o e e e e ; and she continues a a lah ke ase la a a le and the response is ; a a lah. Again she would shout a a nwaaahke aase nwaah le, and the response is a nwaaah. The meaning of this lyrics is that is she clean and the response is that she is clean and the second is enquiring whether she is a virgin or not and the response is that she is a virgin.

There is a gender controversy at this point, namely; the Bafut tradition demands that the girls should go into marriage as virgins and why not the men. In a majority of cases, the men are always the ones who initiates and lures a woman into a romantic dating relationship and when they become pregnant the men are the very ones who not only abandon them but give them a degrading name . That tradition of having girls go into marriage as virgins was possible in the olden days when boys and girls did not interact very easily and the parents chose the wives of their children at a tender age. But nowadays girls and boys spend more time together than with their parents . How possible is it to control what these youths do in their privacy. Apparently this seems very difficult and almost impossible .Nevertheless those who buy the idea of impossibility are definitely choosing the option of losers who would rather prefer that things remain as they are, instead of working hard to fulfill

our responsibilities as reasonable people who have an unswerving desire in finding and pursuing the solution to the problem. In the olden days when almost all respected chastity before marriage and fidelity in marriage, the health situation was good and life expectancy was high. This is the case because family values were highly respected . But presently, individualism which has taken the place of the family, is, in the name of modern life is, promoting body satisfying desires such as free sex and prostitution, laziness and drunkenness homosexuality etc. The consequences of these are very clear even though we pretend not to notice it. This attitude can be explained by the fact that no one is willing to stop what is recognized as the modern way of enjoying life.

At this point it is very pertinent to realize that we are living what Christ revealed in Revelation 2: 20-23 where He makes reference to Jezebel, the prophetess who seduces His servants to commit sexual immorality. There is a serious warning that if she refuses to repent she would contact an incurable disease awaiting her and her accomplishes to end their lives. The number of young people dying of HIV\AIDS is so alarming that if left unchecked would have a very negative impact on the young population. This is the epitome of the providential principle of purity or fruitfulness which, is perfection of character and the principle of restitution or karma. Perhaps the better way to check this is to emphasize on the consequences of the action rather than the do not do it approach. The tradition of the Bafut people that demands purity before marriage is providential.

The outstanding ladies of the grooms family take hold of her, ready to match through the streets with her, proudly proclaiming their marriage to the beautiful, and clean virgin. They will move her through the streets, for all people to admire and continue to their compound where the celebrations would continue until everybody is tired. This will not go as smoothly as described. The young people in the bride's family would from time to time block the way, demanding compensation in the form of money. They do this, expressing disappointment to the fact that they are taking their sister away. Their argument is that they would not let their sister or cousin to go anywhere because they is nobody who can do the work that she does in the house. They are given some small money and they let her go. This is done specifically at the two gates, the one leaving the bride's compound and the other entering the groom's compound. The festivities continue in the groom's compound, with advices from all well wisher on how they can succeed in their marriage until they are tired.

DEATH

The Bafut tradition recognizes death as an important aspect in one's life because it not only marks the beginning of the third stage in one's life but it also ends one's existence in the physical world and begins one's existence in the spirit world. This explains why there are many ceremonies in honor of the departed ancestors. This would be better explained later. The first stage of existence is in water in the mother's womb, followed by that in the land as a physical being combined with a spirit self and finally in the air as a spirit being only. In the early Bafut society that had no external influences, death was a rare event reserved for the old people. If a young person had an accident an d died or became sick and died, it became questionable because it is normal for one to die at an old age. People would go out to consult a soothsayer to know why the young person died and would proceed to have funeral for seven days. Burial takes place depending on the social class of the individual.. The Buntohs or princes and princesses are buried by nkwifor and the celebrations are officially launched by joong. Takumbeng also has a great role to play in the entire celebration. The huge sums of money spent on these have rendered many people bankrupt. Those who feel the impact most are the Bangongs who have become family members as a consequence of marriage. This does not matter to the Buntohs as this poverty would only provide an opportunity for them to insult and ridicule you and blame their sister or brother for marrying such a poor person. Their pride is based on the fact that they as Buntohs would never lack what to eat. Those who suffer are their children and families, most of whom never went to school.

The original concept of giving honor to the departed required that when one dies, mourning takes place for one week . In the case of a christain the church would come for three days and the family would continue for four days. This was the case when there was no mortuary and the diseased was supposed to be buried immediately after death.

Presently, with the coming of the mortuary, most people would prefer to keep their loved ones, who are diseased in the mortuary so that they can take time to prepare a befitting burial for them.

PERIODIC COVERAGE

One day, that is twenty four hours is divided in two periods as identified by the greetings. Abeeh fuoh meh meaning good morning is from day break until noon. Noon will be indicated on a sunny day by the sun overhead. This is when you stand on your shadow. From that time onwards is another period identified by the greetings, oshiemeh, meaning good day.

The weekly period in the Bafut tradition is different from one week in the lunar calendar. There are eight days in the Bafut tradition and seven days in the lunar calendar. thus the traditional days rotate round the lunar calendar days. The eight days are, starting from the most important, Mumita, Mutanibaa, nkufikuu, Ntoobaale, Yika, Yijon, Njwilaa and Mbiindo.

Mumita is the most important day of the week because the first Fon of Bafut died or traditionally known as disappeared on that day, This day became reserved for the Fons, therefore no matter the day on which any Fon disappeared it is announced only on mumita. This is also the traditional Sunday on which many cultural programs take place e g me infor, Successorship, marriages,,cases etc The Fon sits on His throne under the plume tree, close to the most important shrine in the palace to receive all. Everybody is well dressed especially the Princes and Princesses, the Fon's advisers and notables all come out and sit round the Fon for the festivities because there is a lot to drink. Nobody comes to the palace with empty hands, no matter the purpose, so there is always a lot of drinks . Sometimes the Fon's band is there to amuse people ..This day is then reserved for resting and anybody who works could face the wrath of the gods

Mutaniba is considered a minor holiday to enable people get through the fatigue of the previous day.

Yijon is the Fon's market day; that is, the market closest to the Fon's palace. This is the official market day in Bafut . People from all over come to buy from the market.There products in these markets includes ginger, cassava products, notably garri and water fufu, palm products like palm oil, palm wine, and kernels and forest spices from the large virgin forest .

There are two yearly seasons in Bafut known as knoo aloo for the dry season and knoo ntsumben for the rainy season. The rainy season begins in the month of march,that is approximately on March fifteen . April is 'san bwiinfor', meaning the month of the Fon's grass cutting. This is very timely so that the best quality of grass is harvested for the Fon. Every male of age is expected to go to the hill and harvest the young, soft grass for the roofing of grass houses in the palace. The grass is packed according to the various villages so as to facilitate appreciation for yearly awards from the Fon at the end of year festivitiesThe rainy season covers the approximated period March to November. The month of November is known as 'san aloo' that is the beginning of the rainy season. This is also the Takumbeng period, which will be explained later.

December is 'san abene infor., referring to the Fon's annual dance. This is the highest ceremony in the Bafut kingdom.People come home from everywhere to pay homage to ancestors, in the form of dancing. This ceremony takes place for three days. It originated during the reign of HRH Neba Nfor. He was captured in a war in Kom and taken away as a prisoner. This war came as a resujt of the lack of co ordination among the leaders and elders in Bafut. This was the consequence of greed among them.

Nevertheless, just as virtue can never be eliminated, the dexterity of the Fon's guards and the Bukari people made it possible for the Fon to escape. From the arrest. When the Fon arrived home he rewarded his guards and the Bukari people and organized the 'abene infor to celebrate the victory applaud the ancestors for making it possible . This incidence facilitated the co operation between the Mbebeli and the Bukari people. This is signified by the fack sticks that come out with 'ma anforti' and other items of great significance. This has become a very serious cultural event that attracts a lot of tourists and indigenous people from home and abroad.During this event the Fon rewards meritorious people and villages in many aspects as cleanliness of the road network of each quarter, hard work and a variety of others. This serves as a stimulant and everyone works hard to receive these awards and the consequences of this hard work speak for themselves.

This period mobilizes a lot of people into Bafut and economically it can benefit those who can sale to the tourists and others what they want.

There are twelve months of the year in the Bafut traditional calendar namely;
Sang Niboo
Sang Ababe
Sang Ntsembeng
Sang Bui infor
Sang Mikweni

Sang Mandele
Sang Mbu uansanebo
Sang Nkor r njii
Sang Ayo onemfeng
Sang Tsiaber r
Sang Aloo and
Sang Abine

THE BAFUT TRADITIONAL RELIGION

A typical man in Bafut, no matter the era in which he lives, just like other fallen people elsewhere stands for one point at a particular moment and a contrary one a few moments later. This is explained by the fact that fallen man in the fallen world is living in contradiction; the desires of the body opposing the desires of the mind.

Even after the fall of Adam and Eve God did not take away His abode, which is the conscience from them. Thus Adam and Eve after the fall had a good nature originating from the conscience and an evil nature originating from the fallen act . Inhering it from them, in like manner everyone in every society has a positive and a negative side . Therefore it might have been a narcissistic attitude that led the imperial masters to consider the African religious practice as paganic. This might have been the case either because they did not study the traditional values or simply had no time to study what they considered the paganic and primitive values which ought to be replaced with modern values that would facilitate trade and exploitation, which was the principal aim of travelling.

The Bafut traditional religion is very powerful and has been able to survive the mighty influence of modernism in the name of Christianity because it has two aspects, the internal and the external in the subject and object positions, respectively. The internal comprises the good ancestors who live in the spirit world under trees, stones, and water. When they lived on earth, even though they had a fallen nature, they also had more of a good nature and the unswerving desire to develop their fatherland in many aspects and when they died, they continued with those desires. Since they are already in the spirit world, they cannot realize anything on earth unless through somebody who is living on earth. In like manner, Prophet Malachi prophesied that before Christ comes in his first coming, Elijah would have come. But when Christ came and started proclaiming himself as Christ, the superior Jews questioned where Elijah was, for them to believe that he is the real Christ, they have been waiting for. And Jesus who knew everything about the spirit world told them that the coming of Elijah had been realized in the coming of John the Baptist. They would not believe him until John the Baptist confirmed this. But when John the Baptist refused that he is not Elijah, the Jews could also confirmed that he was not Jesus Christ and then went ahead to crucify him. If the spirit of Elijah in the spirit world could work with John The Baptist, how can we be convinced that the spirits of our good ancestors in the spirit world who work with our Ntonwies are demons, as classified by Christianity. It is pertinent to take cognizance of the fact that this was and continuous to be a well calculated plan not only to undermine but to derail and sever the ancestral relationship in order to weaken and take an advantage, just as the sages would say that call a dog a bad name so that you can lynch it. And those who tenacious attached themselves to them took counterproductive moves that had negative impacts on them in the long term but nevertheless God has continued to bless the honest ones to prove that ill-gotten money is not the key to genuine happiness. These ancestors in the spirit world alone know the criteria used in appointing one to serve them as mediums. However in the case of my brother, who is also a Ntonwi one might guess that it is long suffering in innocence .After appointing you, there is training for about two weeks within which time nobody knows where you are. After the training, they come back with a branch of peace trees in their hands and their attire very dirty. Everybody who comes would be told all that had happened and all that would happen in future. They also neutralize evil charms buried in the ground to harm others and at a higher level, they appease the shrines of aggrieved ancestors.

The Ntonwies are the spiritual mediators of the traditional religion who are expected to work in collaboration with the Fon to guard the people to do what their ancestors expect them to do. They call their ancestors who are in the spirit world their gods because they are invisible. The Bafut traditional religion believes in the existence of God as the supreme being and that their ancestors whom they call their gods is only a means through whom they can reach God almighty. One of the pillars of the traditional religion is the pouring of libation and the feeding of their ancestors who dwell under water, trees and stones. The importance of this ceremony is not to be underestimated. Worth noting is the fact that, it recognizes the duality of existence and the fact that the spirit world is in the subject position. It also highlights the principal Trinitarian kingships of human existence namely the parents who represent the present, the children who represent the future and the grandparents who represent the past. The attainment of a successful life or in other words, qualification for entry into the heavenly kingdom, is based on a harmonious give and take relationships that take place in these kingships. It is here that we find the most important institution in the world, which is the family. The family is the first school of love where love is defined as parental love, filial love which is the love that children give to their parents, fraternal love or the love between brothers and sisters and the most important is conjugal love or the love between husband and wife. It is only at this level that love can be consummated. These four types of love are called the four realms of heart as revealed by Rev. Moon. The principal themes that nurture these relationships are respect, obedience, loyalty, support and protection. [Rev. S.M. Moon.

There is a great link that exists between the spirit world and the physical world in the Bafut traditional religion. Even though the parents have died and are in the spirit world, they still continue to interact with people in the physical world. Before the father dies he must appoint his successor and if this is altered it is very certain that terrible things will happen. The successors are expected to work in collaboration with the Ntonwies who are able to communicate with the parents in the spirit world, so that their desire, which is prosperity for all, can be accomplished.

The mediums or ntonwies are able to communicate with those in the spirit world because their spiritual senses are alive. The object they use to link them to the spirit world is their concentrative heart. The distinction between a genuine ntonwi and a native doctor is the fact that the ntonwi has no complicated temples unlike the native doctor who has a very frightful temple that hypnotizes people to believe in them.

I am a living witness to a situation in which one ntonwi saved the victim of witch hunt and explained to him exactly what happened and even called the names of those concerned and the dates and places where this took place. The very amazing fact about this is that the man came from a different Division and they were communicating in English. The Ntonwi I am making reference to here is my senior brother who was one of the most brilliant pioneers of PSS Kumba. As a highly talented young man, he was poisoned and he could not continue with his education. My first experience of this brother is that he is a very honest sick man and it beats my imagination why things happen that way, but nevertheless after serious research I realized that suffering in innocence is blessing in disguise. One summer vacation when I came home, I was informed that he was living in an abandoned house in Nkare Agyati village. I went up there and was determined to discover what was happening. The reaction of one who saw me going up there was, he asked me whether I was not afraid of the mad man staying up there. I asked him whether he ever harmed anybody and the response was that he only shouts in the night but does not harm people. I expressed thanks and continued to meet my smiling brother who gave me a hearty welcome.

There was a dramatic change in his life with weirdness surrounding his utterances and actions. His real mission started in the palace immediately when the Fon died. He was adopted into the Palace when Maanfor realized the importance of the mission he was out to accomplish. When I came home in the early seventies, I can still remember some of the stricking things he said and did. He usually cried out in a loud voice in the night saying very important things. For instance he said that all the evil in Bafut was in a constant and fierce battle with good ancestors, and the outcome is very promising if only the Bafutt people cooperate with the instructions given. He meticulously elaborated on many topics of great importance among which the following would be discussed here.

He concerned himself with the development of Bafut directly initiated by the Ancestors. They are eager to see a positive change in the behavior of people to sacrifice for the purpose of the whole so that these developmental ideals would make Bafut a model kingdom in the North west Region of Cameroon. He was very specific about some foreign friends who were going to open a project for the development of Bafut in infrastructure, roads, small businesses starting with educational conferences. A few years later, The Village Community Project was launched with handsome package that was intended to transform Bafut .

As regards schools, he mentioned the current efforts of some Bafut elites to open colleges in Bafut. He cited some examples specifically as evil because they had foreign connections that were constantly to be in conflict with the culture of the people. He also said the good example is having a missionary connection which will succeed. He even went as far as calling the name of the hill where the college was to settle. He advised the landlords to be understanding because this school, would help the entire Region. And finally COTECC answered this call.

He shouted out about the rehabilitation of some ancestral shrines that were neglected and had become rebellious and harmful such as Mbah and others. He cried out that they were being forced to do the rehabilitation work which needed a lot of money . He explained that it was very painful because nobody was going to understand and it was compulsory for the work to be done. In the later part of 2010 he reported to me that one of the persons who sympathized with the situation and borrowed him with a goat to do the work of rehabilitation of the shrines in Nsem and Agyati, was seriously sick and hospitalized and the money for the goat was needed. I told him that it was a community project, . To be confirmed by the fact that nkwifor is visiting these shrines annually for traditional rituals. We concerted and he made a small bill and sent it to the Nsem Palace. Perhaps they are still planning to do something about it, because when I presented the bill to the Nsem nkwifor they were impressed.

He lamented about the aggrieved spirits of Ndii allah mbweh and Tekore and others that need recognition..

When we realized that they were getting disillusioned because nobody was supporting them, we formed the Foundation for Community Advancement [FOCAD], aimed at encouraging and supporting them because we realized that this project was providentially very important. However the financial support we gave them was limited but however we encouraged them to understand the importance of sacrificing one's self for the sake of others. We could not satisfy their financial demands but did the little we could and also assisted physically, for example in the rehabilitation of Mbah shrine and others and some very deplorable roads like the one linking Niko and Nsem, where we worked manually and mobilized others to work with us as a community project.

They delegated powers to me and I, as secretary of FOCAD in 2007, held a meeting with HRH the Fon of Bafut and Atancho of Nsem where I explained to them who the Ntonwies are and the role they have in the community. The Fon said that the message is correct and that it is for that reason he had given Martin Mabo the red feather, named him Tangang and authorized him to form the Ntonies Foundation . They were eager to know our plans I informed them that we were going to teach the Bafut community the realities of the Bafut Culture and traditional religion.

After this meeting, a new page was opened for FOCAD. Every important project executed was reported to the Fon in writing for example the installation of a bulwark shrine against encroaching enemies in Fonta was reported to the Fon in writing. It is worth noting that perhaps when the Fon gives instructions the contrary is done. In a similar manner, as has always been the case, Tangang, the President of FOCAD, who alone put in place the Fonta shrine, only heard that the same shrine had been innitiated by very powerful herbalists. The wrong thing is always done because these herbalist never communicate with the ancestors and the painful part is that the Ntonwies are compelled by the ancestors to correct all the mistakes made and they is nobody who is willing to help them because they know him as a mad man. This does not change the fact that the ancestors are communicating with him. Therefore the highest personalities of the Bafut traditional religion are the Ntonwi and HRH the Fon and his entourage the second class chiefs .

The next in command in the traditional religion are the Takumbeng. They are they the deacons of the traditional religion. Where ever they are, they are responsible for the respect of cultural norms and in case of violation, the victim is compelled to pay a fine. They are responsible for the construction of ancestral shrines in the community field of each village. Whenever they are doing that, they have the right to feed themselves. Hence on that day, if they cut a plantain, caught a fowl or goat, nobody complains because they are carrying out an official duty.

One of the great traditional religious ceremonies is the community cleansing rituals in grass cutting . This is officiated by the Ntonwies and everybody is expected to bring his own bundle of grass and do exactly as all others are doing. Another traditional religious ceremony is the pouring of libation. This is usually done when there is a celebration and the people are eager to identify and share with their ancestors. An important drink is opened by an important traditional personality after which a presentation is made to the effect that all gathered in the house are milting their differences and desiring to be happy and prosper together. Therefore the good ancestors in the good spirit world are undoubtedly very happy to cooperate. A little portion of the drink is then poured to the floor proclaiming that this is their own portion of the drink. Then at the door facing outside a negative declaration is made. These declarations are very effective. Hence instead of promoting what will impact people negatively a compromising stance is encouraged. Those who come there with a double mind or those who are away in order to sabotage should not be cursed by the evil spirit world but should be taught by the good spirit world to change and become good in order to reap goodness.

Another aspect of the traditional religion is at individual level called 'saafang.' In a very strongly worded and sincere declaration, the concerned states that he/she is innocent and is pleading for protection. Some seniors have special hard small pieces of wood they use for the purpose. This is done several times . This is usually in the case where someone is wrongly accused. This expedites the unfolding of the law of karma, as the Orientals call it or the law of restitution.

Therefore the Bafut traditional religion is a natural law which is an embodiment of the rules and regulations that define the realities of the life of the Bafut people. The central idea is hierarchy, loyalty, respect, obedience, genuineness, severe punishment for transgressors, etc.

However it does not present the ideal, there are repugnant ideals that should not only be frowned upon but discarded, for example lavish expenditures during some funerals and some death celebrations

THE FOUNDATION FOR COMMUNITY
ADVANCEMENT AND THE ECONOMY

FOCAD is highly involved in the economy. This is summarized by what they call, ['Environmental Specificity,' which states that every problem has its solution in its environment of origin.] This applies to many other aspects of life and as far as the economy is concerned, they are saying that the problem of poverty of the Bafut people is to be solved by the Bafut people themselves, using the natural environment they have. It is in this vein that they are encouraging the vulgarization of the palm tree which does very well in Bafut and can provide an answer to the economic situation of the hard working who love it. They are in the process of developing a palm tree nursery of the improved variety which should be able to supply to the farmers who meet a defined criteria for free. This is an important project that requires funding because it has the potential to change the economic situation of Bafut.

In the later part of the nineties and the early two thousand, FOCAD educated Bafut farmers to realize the importance of what they have in their environment. Their awareness was raised on the fact that they should plant what they can consume some and sell the rest for example ginger could be a good fund raiser if well handled and it could also be used as a spice and a common remedy. The farmers were taught improved farming and processing methods of ginger and a variety of other tubers and fruits. These products were presented to an NGO called SAILD and they responded by giving soft loans to the farmers. This money when repaid was going to provide funding to the Bafut Credit House, which would be used to finance other indigenous projects. The abundance of ginger in Bafut today is, thanks to this programme, which even earned for me the name John ginger . Another project of FOCAD and affiliates provided processing equipments, comprising a dehydrator and grinding mill to the Bafut farmers. The aim is to empower them to produce products that can sell at home and abroad .

The most common tree in Bafut is the palm tree. It is to be recognized as one of the most important trees in the Tropics because every part of it has a specific economic value. The majority of these trees in Bafut are planted by rodents. These trees are not even well cared for, consequently their economic value waste away.

The good example of an indigenous who is endeavoring not only to vulgarize but is also meriting the comparative advantage of the palm tree is no other than His Royal Highness Chief Mbonifor of Nsem assisted by his able and industrious wife. They have planted approximately two thousand five hundred palm trees in the Bafut valley. They might not be able to take care of all for shortage of finances but what they take care of is good income for their retirement. If this example impacts others and they do same the economy would improve.

The major theme that runs through the mban is respectful loyalty, payment of allegiance, absolute obedience, and the sharing and redistribution of fortune so that all can live happily.

Mban is the name of a fruit of a very large tree in the forest. All children are called upon to go up the tree and harvest the fruits and bring them to the father.. All the boys and the girls and even the truants are advised to go up the tree and harvest these fruits and bring them to the parents and specifically to His Royal Highness the Fon, because he has no other job than the administration of his people.

The word fruit is literally used here. It symbolizes wealth. All are expected to go out to work and bring the wealth to the king in particular and to the parents in general. The king and the parents are the melting points of all differences in the family. There are weak people in the family who cannot go out to work but as a member of the family they are supposed to have a decent living. The parents are in a good position to collect from those who are strong to share with those who have not. However of greater importance is the fact that the king is not expected to work but to concern himself with administration. Therefore his welfare and that of his family should be the concern of everybody even the criminals. These things are not brought to the center in arrogance but in humility in order to receive blessing. This is reflected in our daily relationship with the palace. Nobody goes to the palace empty handed and expects that his problem would be solved. Neither would anyone come to the father empty handed and expect to receive blessings. Thus the greatest highlight is filial piety and fraternal love comes in as a consequence and in a greater prospective the greatest good for the greatest number through sharing

Thus the mban becomes a pledge of allegiance handed down by ancestors to remind all indigenes of their responsibilities. And when a pledge is made and not respected trouble answers. Thus as we sing the mban each time we should be reminded that we are making a pledge of sharing what we have for the purpose of the whole. And to substantiate that there goes the adage common among the indigenes that we are the ones here and not one alone. This was the communal ideai our ancestors lived before the imperialistic intervention with modernism which gave birth to individualism which has given birth to declarations as," the Bafut man's corn is better for monkeys ", "the young chicken never digs the ground to find food for another."

The issue here is that each time the mban is sung, what every one should understand is that a pledge is being made to uphold the ideal of living for the purpose of the whole. This is the most important aspect of the Bafut tradition which is manifested in many ways for instance in the daily communal interaction when there is a visitor in the house the host would do everything to share the love in the form of something to eat or drink. On the contrary if after making the pledge one turns around to declare that a Bafut mans corn is better for monkeys or better still a young chicken never dicks the ground to find food for another and manifests it by greed, this constitutes a serious contradiction of the ancestral pledge expressed in the mban and thereby creates the missing link with our ancestors known as our gods. The consequence is retrogression. This explains why the Bafut people who violate this find it difficult to attain, maintain and manifest prominence . This will be taken into details for a better unders.tanding subsequently . And in these subsequent editions we would be explaining the beneficial impacts of of the relationship between the Bafut people and the eco-system

And for a final take home, ginger, one of the commonest plants in Bafut has a providential purpose. . Take it as coffee in the morning and evening and you would be amazed with the results.

MBAN

E e e e e kia la kia la

Alume kia mbane

Muma a ngengwen tchia kia mbane ndeh yu kia yu kia

Mugyie nchem tchia kia mbane ndeh yu kia yu kia

A Lum e kia la mu ma a ngweh kia nimu ketu eee

 A Lum ee kia la mbume.

MEANING

We apologize for not using the written Bafut language. This is very useful for development.. Thanks to the efforts of Dr Joseph Nfonyam and others for the accomplishment.

The major themes that run through   include; respectful loyalty allegiance and absolute obedience, unceasing sharing to accomplish filial , fraternal and conjugal love, distribution of fortune so that the weak in the family and society can also have a descent living.

Mban is the name of the fruit of a large tree in the forest , The fruits of this tree are so nutritious that the family can depend on that for days. All the strong ones are called upon to go up the tree , harvest the fruits and bring to the family. All the boys and girls and even the truants are also advised to do same.

This highlights our tradition of sharing what one earns with the family and society leaders so that they as the melting point of all differences can accomplish sanity, order in society and development. This also reminds all that the tradition requires every indigene to share what they earn with HRH The Fon . Hence the traditionally accepted norm that no one goes to the Palace empty hands . And when all is done with humility . blessings follow and you would hear declarations as ,"when you hit your foot against a stone, only the stone will break."

This also reminds us of the traditionally accepted norm of not letting someone come to your house and go without having anything. This is the core value of the society in which our parents lived very happily with out having some people highlydeprived and others living in affluence.

Hence each time we sing the mbane we are reminding ourselves of the pledge of sharing and living for the purpose of the whole and the greaest good for all.

However with foreign intervention and their endeavour to weaken us and take advantage of our resources , a majority of indigens have been nurtured in individualism to the point where not only have they become not onlyso self centered but are so in love with such declarations as a Bafut mans corn is better eaten by monkeys and indeed put this in practice. Isnt this acontradiction of the very pledge we make every time and how do we expects our ancestors to be happy with us.

There are some great ancestors of our kingdom who should be honoured for their great works for the security of our fatherland. The one that comes to mind is Tekore .This is one of our warriors when the Bafut people had to fight against the Germans. He had only one leg and to make himself comfortable in the attack, he dug a hole at a hidden part of the road in Nsem and killed a lot of Germans with poisoned spears arrors and den guns. It is in honour of this hero that there is Atancho of Nsem We are appealing to all of us to develop our ancestry by compiling these great ones and giving the right honor.

Printed in the United States
By Bookmasters